This book was donated to
the New Orleans Public Library
by Nestlé with the support of
Reading Is Fundamental

RIF
Reading Is
Fundamental

Nestlé

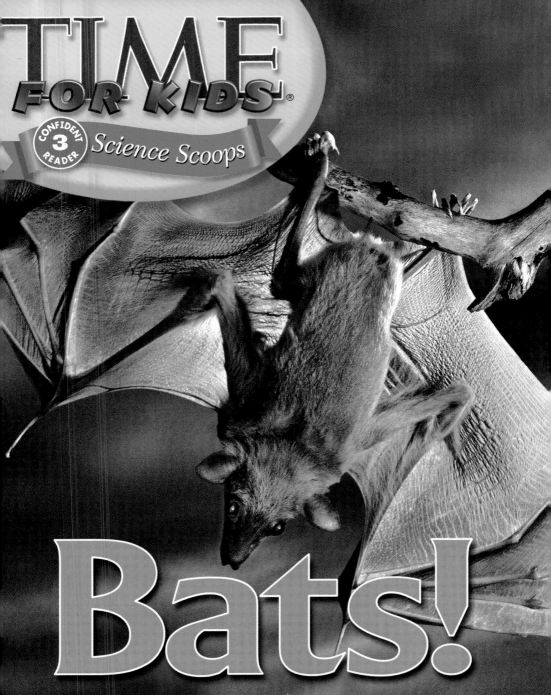

TIME FOR KIDS®

CONFIDENT 3 READER

Science Scoops

Bats!

By the Editors of TIME FOR KIDS
WITH NICOLE IORIO

HarperCollins*Publishers*

About the Author: Nicole Iorio has been educating children for more than a decade, as a teacher and as an editor at TIME FOR KIDS®. She lives in New York with her husband and son. She is also the author of the TIME FOR KIDS® Science Scoops book SPIDERS!

To Jeff, who is a bat-pup savior —N.I.

Special thanks to Barbara French of Bat Conservation International. For more information on this nonprofit organization, please visit www.batcon.org. —N.I.

Library of Congress Cataloging-in-Publication Data is available.

ISBN 0-06-057638-3 (pbk.) — ISBN 0-06-057639-1 (trade)

1 2 3 4 5 6 7 8 9 10
First Edition

Copyright © by Time Inc.
TIME FOR KIDS and the Red Border Design are Trademarks of Time Inc. used under license.

Photography and Illustration Credits:
Cover: Richard Du Toit—Naturepl.com; cover inset: Norbert Wu—Minden Pictures; title page: Bob Elsdale—Getty Images; contents page: Stephen Dalton—Photo Researchers; pp. 4–5: B. G. Thomson—Photo Researchers; pp. 6–7: W. Perry Conway—Corbis; p. 7 (inset): Joe McDonald—Bruce Coleman; pp. 8–9: Barbara Spurll; pp. 10–11: Merlin D. Tuttle—Bat Conservation International; pp. 12–13: Merlin D. Tuttle—BCI/Photo Researchers; pp. 12–13 (inset, top): Charles O'Rear—Corbis; p. 12 (inset): Merlin D. Tuttle—BCI/Photo Researchers; pp. 14–15: IFA Bilderteam/Estock Photo; p. 15 (inset): Theo Allofs—Getty Images; pp. 16–17: Wolfgang Kaehler—Corbis; p. 17 (inset): Barbara Spurll; pp. 18–19: Merlin D. Tuttle—Photo Researchers; pp. 20–21: Merlin D. Tuttle—Bat Conservation International; p. 20 (inset): Juan Manuel Renjifo—Animals Animals; pp. 22–23: Dietmar Nill—Naturepl.com; pp. 22–23 (bottom): Barbara Spurll; pp. 24–25: D. Bruce Means; pp. 26-27: Ken Lucas—Visuals Unlimited; p. 26 (inset): Merlin D. Tuttle—Bat Conservation International; pp. 28–29: Merlin D. Tuttle—Bat Conservation International; pp. 30–31: Steve Kaufman—Corbis; p. 30 (inset): Teh-Sheng Ma; p. 31 (inset): Kevin Schafer; p. 32 (echolocation): Barbara Spurll; p. 32 (mammal): Richard Du Toit—Naturepl.com; p. 32 (nocturnal): Dietmar Nill—Naturepl.com; p. 32 (pollinate): Merlin D. Tuttle—Bat Conservation International; p. 32 (pup): Merlin D. Tuttle—BCI/Photo Researchers; p. 32 (roost): Theo Allofs—Getty Images

Acknowledgments:
For TIME FOR KIDS: Editorial Director: Keith Garton; Editor: Nelida Gonzalez Cutler; Art Director: Rachel Smith; Photography Editor: Jill Tatara

 **Check us out at www.timeforkids.com**

CONTENTS

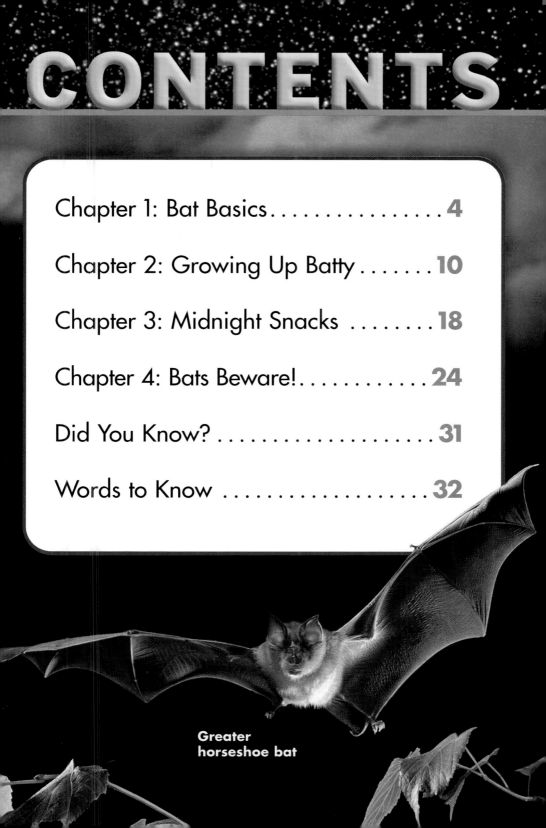

Greater horseshoe bat

CHAPTER ONE

Bat Basics

Ghost bat

Night has fallen. It is time for this little bat to spread its wings and soar away. Like all bats, this creature is nocturnal. It sleeps all day and rises when it is dark. When daylight comes, it folds up its wings and rests.

Bats are mammals.
All mammals have hair and drink milk from their mothers. But bats are different from other mammals in many ways. Bats' bones are lighter. And bats also have wings. So they can do what no other mammals can do. They can fly!

Short-tailed
leaf-nosed bat

Take a look at a bat.

All bats have wings that are much bigger than their bodies. Here are the parts that all bats have in common.

EARS: Bats hear well. Many insect-eating bats have large ears. They can hear sounds that are far away.

EYES: Bats are not blind! They can see well at night.

NOSE: Bats have a good sense of smell. They use their noses to search for food and to locate their babies.

MOUTH: Bats use their mouths for grooming as well as for eating.

BODY: Hair covers the bodies of bats. Some bats have thick fur. Others have thin fuzz.

ARMS: Bats have two arms. An elbow connects the upper arm and forearm.

HANDS: Bats have two hands and can grip objects. Each hand has four long, thin fingers and a thumb. The thumb is short and has a claw.

WINGS: The wings are made of a leathery layer of skin that stretches between the arms and body.

LEGS: Bats have two legs. The knees bend backward, making it easier to crawl quickly.

FEET: When bats rest, they use their clawed feet to hang upside down.

Cuddle time:
fruit bat mothers
and pups

CHAPTER TWO

Growing Up Batty

Bat mothers often gather together to give birth to their babies. In the spring, the air is filled with the chirping of baby bats. Baby bats are called pups.

Flying fox
mother
and pup

Pups depend on their mothers.
They drink their mothers' milk. Some pups
fly with their mothers as they hunt. Others
wait at home for food.

Flying
together:
a fruit bat
and pup

Bats grow up fast. A pup loses its baby
teeth when it is only ten days old! At a
month, the pup is strong enough to fly.
At a year, a bat is all grown up.

Bats live in homes called roosts.
They give the bats shelter from the weather, protection from enemies, and a place to rest. Caves and trees are favorite roosts. But bats also live in attics and cellars and under bridges. They live all over the world, except where it is very cold.

Flying fox
bats rest by
hanging from
tree branches.

HANG TIME!

Flying
fox

There are more than one thousand different kinds of bats. Most have black, brown, or gray fur. The dark color helps keep them hidden in the night sky. But bats that rest outside during the day are sometimes a bright color. They may be orange, red, white, or spotted.

How Big?

The flying fox of Indonesia is the world's biggest bat. It can weigh three and one half pounds and has a six-foot-wide wingspan. That's wider than a car! The bumblebee bat of Thailand is the world's smallest bat. It has a three-inch-wide wingspan.

CHAPTER THREE

Midnight Snacks

After a good day's
sleep, bats are hungry.
Bats that live in tropical
areas feast on fruit and
flowers. They rely on their sharp
senses of sight and smell to find
their meals. Bats drink syrupy
nectar from flowers. They dig into
sweet berries, bananas,
mangoes, and other fruit.

YUM!

Long-nosed bat

A lesser bulldog bat eats a fish.

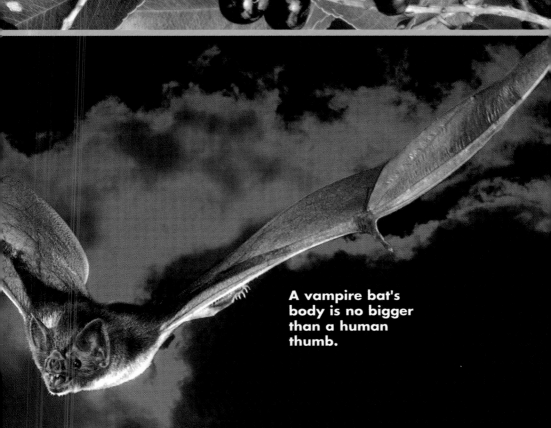

A vampire bat's body is no bigger than a human thumb.

Some bats are meat eaters.

They eat fish, frogs, lizards, mice, and birds. Sharp claws and teeth help meat-eating bats catch and eat their prey.

Vampire bats are found in Central and South America. They drink blood from animals without killing their prey. These bats bite cows, pigs, and chickens, and lick the blood from the

Watch out, bugs!

Most bats are on the lookout for insects. An insect-eating bat can eat half its weight in just one night. That could be hundreds of bugs! A bat scoops up bugs as it soars through the air. It uses a special kind of hearing called echolocation to find food.

GOTCHA!

A greater horseshoe bat catches a moth.

Echo

Sound wave

A SPECIAL SENSE

Echolocation is a sense that helps bats find and catch prey. Bats produce very high sounds. These sound waves travel through the air. They hit an object. Then an echo is reflected back. If the echo is soft, the bat knows the object is far away. If the echo is strong, the object is close.

CHAPTER FOUR

Bats Beware!

Bats must watch out for large predators. Hawks, falcons, owls, and other birds snatch bats from the night sky. Frogs, cats, raccoons, foxes, and snakes hunt bats on the ground.

A green tree frog gobbles a bent-wing bat.

Ozark bats
are rare.

Humans are the biggest threat to bats.

People cut down trees and destroy bats' roosts. They use chemicals in farming that harm bats. There are endangered bats in many parts of the world.

The Rodrigues fruit bat is one of the most endangered bats in the world.

Bats are not spooky!

They don't spread disease. And they don't drink people's blood! Bats usually avoid people. Fewer people die each year from bat bites than from bee stings.

Bats are helpful. They eat insects that destroy crops. They also pollinate flowers and spread seeds. People around the world are working to save bats.

A flying fox licks pollen from a coral tree.

Bat fans gather at Congress Street Bridge in Texas to watch Mexican free-tail bats.

Batwoman to the Rescue!

Barbara French is a bat scientist. She works for a group called Bat Conservation International. She has taken care of animals since she was a child.

French became batty for bats when she visited the Congress Street Bridge in Austin, Texas. It is famous for the bats that roost there. "A huge cloud of bats flew out from under the bridge," says French. "It was just the most exciting thing."

French fixes broken wings, makes bug shakes for thirsty bats, and helps pups learn to fly. Her work has taught her that bats are social creatures. "They do a lot of talking," she says.

Did You Know?

- Bats are not related to birds.

- Some bats in Central America live in tents made of leaves.

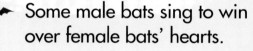

Tent making bat

- One quarter of all mammals are bats.

- Some male bats sing to win over female bats' hearts.

- One kind of West African bat lives in spiderwebs.

- Texas is home to the most bats in the United States.

WORDS  to Know

Echolocation: an ability to use sound waves to locate an object; the waves are reflected back to the sender

Pollinate: to spread powdery pollen so new flowers will grow

Mammal: an animal that has hair and drinks milk from its mother

Pup: a baby bat

Nocturnal: being active during the night

Roost: a place where bats rest

FUN FACTS

TOP 5 FOODS BATS EAT

1

Insects
774 kinds of bats eat insects

2

Fruits and Flowers
316 kinds of bats eat fruit and nectar

3

Animals
8 kinds of bats eat small animals

4

Fish
4 kinds of bats eat fish

5

Blood
3 kinds of bats drink blood from animals